WHAT HAPPENS DURING AN ECLIPSE?

Astronomy Book Best Sellers
Children's Astronomy Books

BABY PROFESSOR

EDUCATION KIDS

Speedy Publishing LLC

40 E. Main St., #1156

Newark, DE 19711

www.speedypublishing.com

Copyright 2017

In this book, we're going to talk about the two types of eclipses, lunar and solar. So, let's get right to it!

WHAT IS AN ECLIPSE?

If you are an observer on Earth, an eclipse happens when light from a celestial body is covered over by another object passing through the path of the light.

There are two types of eclipses that we see on Earth, an eclipse of the Moon, called a lunar eclipse, and an eclipse of the Sun, called a solar eclipse.

WHEN DOES AN ECLIPSE HAPPEN?

During a lunar eclipse, the Earth gets between its satellite, which is the Moon, and the Sun. The Moon doesn't produce any light by itself. It just reflects the light that comes from the Sun. So, when the Earth gets in the way, it blocks part of the light from the Sun's rays from reflecting off the Moon. When the lunar eclipse is happening, you see a shadow being cast over the Moon's surface from the Earth.

During a solar eclipse, the Moon gets in the way of the Earth's line up with the Sun. When this occurs, the Sun's light can't get to us for a short time. The sky gets darker as the Moon gradually gets lined up in front of the rays of the Sun. If the Moon and the Sun get in perfect alignment, which just means they are totally lined up, it is a total eclipse of the Sun.

The Moon is much, much smaller than the Sun. However, the Moon is much closer to the Earth than the Sun so that's why it can "cover over" the light from the Sun. It's a good thing that the Moon doesn't block the light from the Sun all time, because if it did we'd never have a sunny day.

UNDERSTANDING THE MOON'S PHASES

The Moon is Earth's natural satellite. This just means that the Moon orbits or goes around the Earth. It makes one complete orbit around the Earth every 29-1/2 days.

As it goes around our planet, it changes position in relationship to the Sun. This change in position causes the Moon to go through phases. From Earth, we see these different phases as the Moon changes shape every night. There are eight different phases. The only one we can't see is the New Moon because that's when the bright side of the Moon is pointed away from Earth's view.

Ever since people looked up into the sky, they've been fascinated with the Moon's changing phases. The pattern of seeing the Moon change in a regular way helped primitive people mark the passage of time. Some cultures have calendars that begin and end depending on the Moon's phases. The Chinese calendar as well as the Hebrew and Muslim calendars are set up this way. The New Moon is always at the beginning of the month and the Full Moon is mid-month.

During the phase when there's a Full Moon, it shows up during the time of sunset and can be seen all night. When the night ends, it sets when the Sun comes up. No other phases of the Moon work this way. It happens due to the fact that when the Moon is full, it falls in a straight line opposite to the Sun's position. The Full Moon phase is important to lunar eclipses.

THE EARTH'S SHADOW

Lunar eclipses only happen during the Full Moon phase and they only happen when it's positioned so that it passes through a part of Earth's shadow. Earth's shadow is actually made up of two different distinct shadows. They are each inside each other.

The outer shadow is called the penumbral shadow. This shadow blocks some, but not all, of the light from the Sun from the Moon's surface.

The inner shadow is called the umbral shadow. This shadow prevents any sunlight from getting to the Moon's surface.

TYPES OF LUNAR ECLIPSES

There are three distinct types of eclipses of the Moon.

- ⊙ Penumbral
- ⊙ Partial
- ⊙ Total

Penumbral: This type of eclipse is difficult to see, even with a telescope. This event occurs when the Moon goes through the path of the penumbral shadow. About 35% of all lunar eclipses are this type.

Partial: During this type of lunar eclipse, a part of the Moon goes through the umbral shadow. These types of eclipses are simple to observe even without a telescope. About 30% of all lunar eclipses are this type.

Total: The whole Moon goes through the umbral shadow. These types of eclipses are easy to see with the naked eye and exciting to watch since the Moon turns red when it's in the total phase. About 35% of all lunar eclipses are this type.

WHY DOES THE MOON TURN RED?

During a total lunar eclipse, indirect sunlight still gets to the Moon and reflects off of it. However, the light needs to pass through our atmosphere, which filters out most of the blue color. This is why the Moon looks orange or deep red.

OBSERVING LUNAR ECLIPSES

It's completely safe to watch a lunar eclipse unlike a solar eclipse. You can see it clearly even without binoculars or a telescope.

HOW OFTEN DO LUNAR ECLIPSES OCCUR?

Astronomers have calculated how many partial and total lunar eclipses there have been and will be within the five thousand year period of 2000 BC to 3000 AD. The number is 7,718 eclipses. If you're interested in viewing a total or partial lunar eclipse you can find this chart online and plan when you'll be watching the sky.

WHAT'S THE DIFFERENCE BETWEEN THE TWO TYPES OF ECLIPSES?

A solar eclipse is when the Moon blocks our view of the Sun. A solar eclipse can only happen during the New Moon phase of the Moon's cycle during the time when the Moon is positioned between the Earth and the Sun.

The New Moon happens once in every 29-1/2 day cycle, but it doesn't always eclipse the Sun because of the different tilts of the orbits. Twice a year or more, the three celestial bodies line up just right so that the moon blocks the way the Sun looks.

Just like the Earth's shadow has two parts, the Moon's shadow also has two parts.

Penumbra, this is the outer shadow of the Moon, which is pale

Umbra, this is the inner shadow of the Moon, which is dark

When the Moon's outer shadow hits Earth, we're able to see a partial eclipse of the Sun from that area. You have to be very careful to look at a partial solar eclipse because the part of the Sun that's not covered over is very bright and can damage your eyes. You'll need a special filter or a pinhole projector to look at a partial eclipse of the Sun.

WHAT IS THE PATH OF TOTALITY?

If the Moon's inner shadow hits the Earth, then the result is a total eclipse of the Sun. The track of the Moon's inner shadow as it travels across the Earth is called the Path of Totality.

This path is about 10,000 miles in length but its width is only about 100 miles. That means if the Path of Totality travels across the United States only people in certain states, in a very specific area within those states, would witness the solar eclipse as a total eclipse.

If you witnessed a total solar eclipse in City A, you'd have to wait an average of 375 years or so to see it again from that same exact location. Depending on the city, you might only have to wait 65 years, whereas in another location it might be 600 years.

The total blackout of the Sun by the Moon during a solar eclipse only lasts for a few fleeting minutes. It is amazing to witness though. The sky seems like twilight although it's day. Surrounding the black Moon that is blocking the Sun's rays is the part of the Sun it can't cover—the solar corona.

The corona is composed of super-hot plasma that's over two million degrees Fahrenheit. The only time the corona can be seen is when the Sun is completely covered by the Moon's "face."

When viewing or photographing a solar eclipse, it's important to have the right equipment so you won't damage your eyes in the process of observing.

There are four different types of solar eclipses:

Total, the Sun is completely obscured by the Moon and observers in the Path of Totality will witness a total eclipse

Annular, the Moon masks the Sun but the Sun can still be seen around the Moon's edges

Partial, the Sun is only partially blocked by the Moon

Hybrid, under rare conditions a total eclipse can transform into an annular eclipse or an annular can change into a total somewhere along the eclipse path

Astronomers have calculated the number of solar eclipses from 2000 BC to 3000 AD and there are 11,898 in total of all of the different types.

Awesome! Now you know more about what eclipses are and how they happen. You can find more Astronomy books from Baby Professor by searching the website of your favorite book retailer.

CPSIA information can be obtained
at www.ICGtesting.com
Printed in the USA
LVOW05s0041090817
544317LV00004B/12/P